A SINGLE DROPLET
Finding Freedom Through Daily Practice

T O R E Y   H I L L

BALBOA.PRESS
A DIVISION OF HAY HOUSE

Balboa Press books may be ordered through booksellers or by contacting:

Balboa Press
A Division of Hay House
1663 Liberty Drive
Bloomington, IN 47403
www.balboapress.com
844-682-1282

Print information available on the last page.

ISBN: 979-8-7652-4548-4 (sc)
ISBN: 979-8-7652-4550-7 (hc)
ISBN: 979-8-7652-4549-1 (e)

Library of Congress Control Number: 2023917482

Balboa Press rev. date: 10/20/2023

PRAISE FOR *A SINGLE DROPLET*

"We're all given the gift of life and in that gift comes tricks and mirages and thousands of ways to sabotage our incredible ability to shine bright. Those meanderings are where the good in us becomes magnificent. In these gracious pages, Torey gives her readers pathways and tools to witness how naturally extraordinary we all are, whilst holding you in her arms the entire way."

- Adrea L. Peters, award-winning author and entrepreneur

"Torey is a skillful and deeply authentic guide. She understands what people need to feel a greater sense of personal connection, ease and grace in their lives. Her words are mesmerizing, and *A Single Droplet* will speak directly to the heart of all who read it."

- Kate Snowise, Professional Coach & Podcaster

"*A Single Droplet* is a kind, trusted companion designed to help you find your way home. Poetic, beautifully real and filled with evidence-based pearls of wisdom, Torey's mindfulness and self-care practices are the perfect antidote to modern life. Her invitation to slow down, reconnect with who you are and care deeply for your body, mind and soul is just what we need. This couldn't have come at a better time. Brave and kind, I love this gem of a book. Bravo Torey, well done!"

- Renee Trudeau, catalyst/retreat facilitator and author "Nurturing the Soul of Your Family: 10 Ways to Reconnect & Find Peace in Everyday Life."

CONTENTS

DISCLAIMER

The information in this book does not substitute as medical advice. The reader is encouraged to contact appropriate medical support for diagnosis, treatment, and prevention in regards to physical and mental health concerns. The content in this book discusses mental illness and may be triggering for some readers. Please take care of yourself as needed.

A SINGLE DROPLET

A young girl stands at the edge of a small pond
Among tall grass and wildflowers
Green rolling hills in the distance
Thick clouds above

She listens to the birdsong and buzzing wings of the dragonfly
A gentle breeze brings the smell of rain to her nostrils
Goose bumps appear across her bare arms
She watches the water as it mirrors the darkening sky

Suddenly her gaze is drawn to the center of the pond
As soon as the splash catches her eye, it disappears
Unwilling to blink, delighted by what is to come
She waits for the show to start

The rings begin to form
One after another
From the middle, extending outward

Gently rocking the lily pads floating on the water's surface
Sending a small whisper to the salamanders below
Tickling plants that live at the outer edge
Vibrating the reflection of the clouds

Eyes locked until the water smooths over once more
Turning her body, she walks away
In awe of the world's wonders
How a single droplet could create something so much bigger
than itself

THE BREAKING POINT

I linger in the waiting room, flipping through old magazines and eavesdropping on other's muffled conversations, when suddenly I hear, "Victoria!" Always slightly embarrassed when people use my full name, I obediently get up and make my way toward the voice. I am led around the corner and invited into a small office, lounge chair to the left, a swivel chair to the right. My eyes glance out the large window overlooking the outdoor stairs, parking lot, and pine trees. I'm anxious, oblivious to the smaller objects scattered around the room, my mind moving faster than my eyes can see.

I sit in the lounge chair; it's clearly for me, the patient. I cross my legs, hoping this makes me look confident, and make eye contact with my new counselor, a short, middle-aged woman with curly dark hair. I'm ready to tell her everything because I am ready to be fixed. I'm here to patch myself back together and I want it done yesterday.

After we introduce ourselves and politely chat for a few moments, I dive into why I'm here: intrusive thoughts, looping thought patterns, and high anxiety. I don't care that this woman is a stranger. I don't mind sharing my issues. I've seen other therapists; this isn't new to me. I figure the sooner I spill it all, the sooner she can give me the solution I so desperately seek. I'm tired of feeling scared of my own thoughts. I'm exhausted fighting with myself every minute of every day. I need the panic attacks to stop finding me on vacations and in meetings at work. I need to be able to trust myself again and not get sucked into the dark vacuum of my imagination. My knuckles are white, trying to hold all the strings of myself together, as if I'm clinging to a hundred balloons that are whipping around in high wind. I need to be fixed. I *need* this woman to fix me.

After sharing my mental health history, I tell her I've been able to get better every time something hard has come up. "I can handle myself," I say to her, and I think about the little flame inside of me. No matter how dark it gets in my mind, this flame never goes out. I've always felt it—the willingness to keep moving forward. Later in life a good friend would explain that this is *resiliency*.

"These thoughts and anxieties come and go," I continue, "but the reason I'm sitting in this chair is because they always return. I want them to stop. I want the fear to go away. I need peace."

I try to explain the process of my brain. "It's like playing Whac-A-Mole. Every time I think I'm better, the unwanted thoughts come back, disguised in a new mask, taking me for another roller-coaster ride. I want to get *off* the roller coaster. I need to get off."

I finish bringing her up to speed and she responds with a sly smile. "Spoken like a lady with OCD," she says. My heart stops and a lump grows deep inside my throat. The blood drains from my face as I feel full-on defense rising up from within, a combination of fury and heartbreak, swallowing me whole.

How does this stranger say something so bold and life-altering only halfway into our *first* session together . . . and so matter-of-factly? How dare she label me? How can she overlook *all* the work I've done, *all* the things I've overcome? As I had told her, I could have easily spun-out into a life of chaos and self-destruction. But I've held onto every single string. I've kept myself and my life—my really full and healthy life—together. Intact. Doesn't that count for something?

My mind went on . . . Does *she* know what it's like to hold onto oneself like this? How exhausting it can be? How unsettling and lonely? Doesn't she know that a label like that can destroy someone? Make them feel completely hopeless? Like the work they've done doesn't matter? That they should just let go of every single string and give up? What's the point of holding on if you're doomed to begin with?

I'm a lost cause, I tell myself. And at that, I drop my head into my hands and sob.

DEDICATION

To the person whose inner flame remains lit through harsh wind and moonless nights.

For the dreamer, lost in the woods at dusk—

> —who walks into the unknown; led by something larger than themself; ready to choose courage, again and again; trusting that curiosity is their compass and fear is always smaller than it feels; knowing that the path they walk is uniquely their own; that there is no box they could squeeze themself into. It would tear.

I dedicate this to *you*.

MY STORY

As a little girl, I would watch my family members intently, in tune with their tones of voice, facial expressions, and even the pace of their steps as they walked around the house. Based on my observations, I transported their emotions into my own little body, taking on their sadness, anger, joy, and love.

In grade school, a close friend of mine became ill and had to stay in the hospital for a few nights. My mom drove me and another friend to visit her. During the car ride I wondered what my sick friend must be feeling. Once we arrived and found her room, one of the first things I said was, "I'm so sorry this is happening. It must feel like a nightmare that you wish you could wake up from."

My friend looked at me with wide eyes and said, "That's *exactly* how I feel."

I always thought this was a superpower: to be able to feel what others were feeling. But to be this in tune with others can be dangerous. It can trick you into thinking that, if you can feel everything, you should be able to fix it all too. As a young child, and even through adolescence, I poured a lot of myself into the well-being of others, taking on their responsibility to feel and live well. I tried so hard but never felt like it was enough.

I didn't know then that I do not hold the power to make such intimate decisions for others, that I cannot walk someone else's path.

If I could travel back in time, I'd walk up to my nine-year-old self, crouch down, lock eyes with her, place my hands gently on each cheek, and whisper, "Your only job is to make sure that you feel all the love inside. All that love in you, it's like the sun! It'll shine out onto others and warm them up too. This is the best way to help them, to love yourself well."

In parallel with this soft and insightful little girl, I was also *wild*. I ran around my home and yard, often naked, splashing around the flooded grass beneath thunderstorms, searching for toads to play with. I refused to wear shoes during the summer, which resulted in black feet with thick calluses that allowed me to charge over rocks and across hot pavement. I swam in fresh bodies of water for hours, eyes wide open without the protection of goggles, only coming up for air when I absolutely needed to.

My brothers and I played rough, racing around the lawn and knocking things over in the house. I'd climb high up in our old cedar tree, perch on my favorite branch, and make strange animal sounds at Ruth, our beloved elderly neighbor across the street. She would look around, from below in her driveway, utterly confused, and concerned about what type of animal could be lurking nearby. This untamed spirit pounded like a drum in my chest, always demanding more space to roam.

Then there was my imagination, my boundless and relentless imagination, that ran as wild as my body did. I wanted to see beyond where my feet could take me. So, I brought myself there through make-believe. I daydreamed about fairies and conjured up other worlds to play in. I caused trouble with my imaginary friend, Sara, once ripping off a section of wallpaper in my bedroom and blaming it on her. I was furious when my mother punished me and not Sara.

At night, I laid in bed, paralyzed by the frightening images that appeared in my mind. Sometimes my imagination took me to places I didn't want to go to.

During car rides, I was consumed with intangible realities, like outer space and death, blowing my young mind with the vastness and impermanence of life. My eyes would glaze over and I'd be transported out into the galaxy, where I could see earth as a speck in the distance, and wonder if that's where I'd go when I died, back into the stars. Just as I could jump into other people's emotions, I could wrap my head around the magnitude of *life*.

As an adult, in current time, I feel these traits running through my veins, alive and well. I am still deeply sensitive, but have developed an awareness that alerts me when I am traveling into other people's emotions. I still swim far out into fresh bodies of water, only coming up for air when I absolutely need to. I howl deep in the woods, running on trails pretending I'm a wolf, sometimes accidently calling in real coyotes. And I still imagine—wondering what *could* be—my mind floating and seeking and playing.

But in the space between childhood and adulthood, my story runs rather dark. Through adolescence and my early twenties, I suffered and struggled. My sensitivity for others became overbearing, my wildness muted, and my imagination disfigured. The things that made me *me* became tangled and lost. *I* was lost.

In middle school, anxiety began to consume me, creeping in closer and closer, eventually causing root rot where healthy life once grew. My days became heavy with shame and irrational worry. I didn't know what was going on inside me because so many feelings were happening at once. And they weren't clear, but more like a messy blob of gray overlapping watercolors on a flooded piece of white paper. I felt disoriented and out of control.

It was like I was swimming in the middle of an ocean, looking for pieces of rubble to keep me afloat. When I found one, I'd grab it and hoist my upper half onto it, then lie with relief, but only for a moment. Eventually, the object would sink beneath my weight. I'd drop back into the cold water and frantically seek something else to cling to, my eyes wild with fear, and my body slow with exhaustion.

All I could do was react—which actually offered some short-term relief. Validation from others and strict control over my weight became my lifelines. This brief and temporary respite allowed my mind to believe that validation and weight control made me feel better. The problem is that the external world is only guaranteed to shift and change; it is unlikely to offer stable ground for long.

I now know that some people will like me, and others will not; relationships will change over time. My weight will fluctuate as I live through four seasons each year and enter different seasons of my life. But back then, it was an exhausting effort seeking refuge in these temporary solutions, keeping myself afloat this way.

At eighteen, I left my small Vermont hometown of Windsor for Burlington to attend the University of Vermont (UVM). The small city of Burlington sits on a big lake, tucked inside the rolling mountains of northwestern Vermont. It is ruled by students, with different college campuses dispersed across the city and run-down housing rentals in almost every residential neighborhood. In the heart of downtown, there is a pedestrian-only brick street lined with local shops, farm-to-table food, street talent, and bars humming with the music of bands playing inside.

Only a few blocks away is Lake Champlain, one of the largest bodies of water in the United States, connecting Vermont, New York, and Quebec. Sailboats weave between the scattered islands. I used to run from my apartment to the local lookouts just to catch the dazzling sunsets over the lake. I still run to these lookouts when I visit.

In Burlington, I found the spaciousness and freedom to figure out who I was. The little city whispered to me as I walked through it, daring me to show more, to shed my protective layers, and embrace my authentic self. It was like I had been wearing the same jeans since sixth grade back in Windsor. Over time, they'd become so soft, so paper thin, that I didn't notice how tight they gripped my flesh, the metal button leaving a permanent dent in my belly. I had outgrown these jeans years ago, and only now was I realizing it.

During this time, however, I found myself stuck between two versions of myself: version one—the high-school Torey, trapped inside harmful, looping thought patterns, with low self-esteem and limiting beliefs, desperately trying to numb and manage the chaos inside; and version two—the new, adventurous, and extroverted hippy-child, inspired by the freedom and unlimited possibility at her fingertips.

Nobody tells you that you don't just change from one version to the next, that there's an awkward and sometimes painful transition period between the two. Like a moth tirelessly hatching from its sticky cocoon, or a snake trying to wiggle out of its itchy skin. On the cusp of new, but gripped by the old, I'd teeter back and forth between these two selves. They coexisted like two incompatible roommates. I was a free-spirited—and lost—young woman.

Yet, as my college experience progressed, the fear I had cultivated for so long had a new opponent: hope. Hope—that I could one day fully be myself. Hope—that I could discover her, let her surface, and love her, unconditionally. I was getting a taste of what the true Torey felt like, behind the angst and insecurities. And I wanted *more*. Life felt free and fun with her around. I began to feel my energy and spirit come back to life, like a bear climbing out of its den and into the sunshine at the end of a long winter.

This led me to question the validity of the fear-based thoughts that had ruled my life for so many years. Had they been lies all along? Did I *need* to be overly nice to others, to put their interests, opinions, and stories above mine, in order to be likable? Did I *need* to use so much humor and high energy for new people to consider being my friend? Did I *need* to hide my anxiety when it surfaced, stuffing it back down and plastering a permanent smile across my face, so as to not disrupt the vibe of a friend group? Did I *need* to rehearse my words over and over inside my head before feeling confident enough to raise my hand in class? Were all the questions I wanted to ask about course material really stupid, or would they have helped, not only me, but others too? Did I *need* to weigh a certain number to feel beautiful? Did I *need* to fix others in order to be lovable? With each question, the cement wall around my heart began to crack and crumble.

I became liberated by the idea that there was something bigger than my fear and judgment. Slowly I felt my hopeful inner flame heighten, and strength rise from my core. And with that, I took action. I made an appointment with a counselor on campus, opened up my journal, and said *yes* to things that threw me outside my comfort zone.

During my junior year, I forced myself to take a public speaking course—my literal nightmare. This wasn't a requirement of my major, or even my minor, but I had heard a friend talking about how this class had helped them with their confidence. So, with a frog-like gulp, I convinced myself that I must do it too. Shaky *and* inspired, I made it through this class. And then I surprised even myself by taking on the role of teacher's assistant (TA) for two more semesters, guiding others through their own public speaking journeys.

During the same time, I took on another TA role, in my favorite anthropology course. One day the professor asked me to lead the lecture. She sat to the side as I introduced new material to the students while standing at the front of the large classroom. I was more terrified than I'd ever been, full of impostor syndrome. They're all smarter than you, Torey, I thought. You are embarrassing yourself.

The professor recognized my discomfort. After class, when everyone else was gone, she smiled into my eyes and told me that women are allowed to take up space, and that we must learn how to do so. Her tone was compassionate yet stern, instilling a sort of confidence in me. It was like she had written a permission slip, a reminder that I too had the right to be seen and heard. I had the right to stand in front of that classroom, just as she did.

As I proved more and more of my limiting beliefs and fears wrong, the mysteries of *me* began to reveal themselves. I learned to rely on myself and enjoy my own company. I walked alone through the vibrant markets of Oaxaca City during my study abroad experience sophomore year. Making my way up and down unfamiliar streets with nobody by my side, I don't know which felt more foreign: the strong smells of raw meat and sauteed crickets or my own company.

Once back on UVM's campus, junior year, I found an unexpected passion for poetry through an assignment in Spanish class; my ears still ring with my professor's words after reading my work aloud, *¡Ahhh, una poetisa!* The following year, the same professor would award my Global Studies senior term paper with a publication that only a handful of students earn. This external validation uncovered something deep within me, a sense of worthiness, offering me a place at the table.

On graduation day, I walked my family toward a building where a small gathering was being hosted for the students who had earned that publication. As we were weaving through the crowds of grads and families, we ran into the anthropology professor I had been a TA for. I eagerly introduced her to my parents. She greeted them and went on to say how smart their daughter was. I was stunned by these words leaving the mouth of a Harvard graduate and esteemed college professor. I had dedicated four years of myself at UVM, often believing that I was less than everyone else there, that I didn't belong. How wrong I was.

THE MISSING INGREDIENT: DAILY PRACTICE

After graduating, my now-husband, Jake, and I crammed all our belongings into one vehicle and hit the road. For two years, we lived in Salt Lake City, Utah, and then spent one more in Portland, Oregon. On weekends, and between moves and new jobs, we covered thousands of miles across the United States and Canada. We stargazed in the Moab desert countless times, popping champagne on the red rocks during sunsets with our friend group, our family away from home. We nestled in our sleeping bags, listening to moose walk around our campsite in the Tetons. We witnessed gray whales spouting off the coast of Olympic National Park, walked a tad too close to grazing buffalo in Yellowstone (and lived to tell the tale), skied the Wasatch Mountain Range, trudged through the narrows in Zion, surfed the Oregon coast, hiked through British Columbia with bear spray in our back pockets, and adopted our sweet dog, Ziggy. Here I was, finally living a life that honored my wanderlust spirit.

But I could not shake that lingering darkness deep within. Even in the best of my memories, I recall this heavy feeling of unease. I was always watching my back. But it was *me* I was afraid of. Old thought patterns clung to me, refusing to let go, trapping me as if they were a weighted net, and I, their prey. I worried all the time, about everything, turning over every rock, looking for potential catastrophe.

I remember hiking along the Oregon coast one day in a full panic. Nothing bad had happened. The sun was shining and we had camped under the stars the night before. I didn't know how to tell Jake that I felt like I was going to die, that something awful was going to happen . . . because *nothing* was wrong. I couldn't articulate out loud something I didn't know how to explain to myself.

In such moments, I found relief in knowing that I would someday die. It wasn't that I wanted my life to end, but knowing that it would, brought me some sort of comfort. I felt relief in this inevitable truth, a light at the end of the tunnel.

Looking back, I see that my despair was caused by this forever daily battle with mental illness. Instead of finding appropriate support or focusing on something other than my anxiety-based thoughts, I threw on a helmet, grabbed my weapons, and marched up to the face of my opponent.

I do not now criticize my former self for doing this. It makes perfect sense why I would try so hard to defeat the thing causing my problems. But I eventually learned that this approach was a never-ending roller-coaster ride, one with no seat belt and too many sharp turns. It was the same cyclical process, over and over again. A fearful thought would pop into my mind, I would defeat it, and in would walk a new one. Although exhausted, I had accepted this as my forever reality . . . until I hit my breaking point a few years later in the counselor's office.

• • • • •

When I got home, on the night of my OCD diagnosis—as in obsessive-compulsive disorder—I dropped my work bags on the ground, plopped onto the couch, sunk my head into my hands, and broke down, again. I felt hopeless and defeated and tired.

But there it was, buried deep inside, below the heavy darkness: a faint glow of wonder, a gentle curiosity encouraging me to find *my* solution. There had to be one, I thought, as that warm flicker of resilience lit up inside.

In this moment of contradictory feelings, hopelessness and hope, I did the first thing that came to mind: find a podcast about anxiety. This semiconscious instruction felt random. I had never listened to a podcast before.

But I took a chance on this intuitive hit and scrolled through the anxiety podcasts until one caught my eye. I clicked on the beginning episode and pressed Play. After listening to the first couple minutes, tears of relief began to roll down my cheeks. It felt like the host was speaking directly to me, as if she knew exactly how I was feeling and, more importantly, she seemed to know how to help.

With each word, I felt less alone, less out of control. I had found someone to walk alongside me as I trekked up my own jagged mountain. It didn't matter that she wasn't with me in real time. It didn't even matter that she had no idea who I was. What mattered was that I felt seen *and* there were actionable steps I could take to help myself. In this moment, I started to believe that I could feel better, that I had some agency over my situation. Tears dried on my cheeks as I found inspiration through someone else's words.

The following day, during my morning commute, I listened to the next episode. I finished out the week like this: jumping into a new ritual, feetfirst. Days turned to weeks, weeks turned to months, and to this very day, you'll find me listening to podcasts in my little white Subaru hatchback. Something momentous happened here, something way beyond the discovery of podcasts.

• • • • •

Once I had established this new daily practice, I became inspired to add other small tweaks into my days. On that drive to work, I'd also repeat memorized mantras out loud and reflect on what I was grateful for in that moment. During my lunch break, I'd drive to a nearby trailhead, throw on my sneakers, and go for a short nature walk. After work, I'd stop at the gym and get my heartrate up before heading home. When I saw an opportunity, I'd step outside my comfort zone or commit a random act of kindness. I began to prioritize self-care and attempted to slow down a bit. Every time a new practice took form, another began to unfold, leading me down a path of curiosity and relief.

At the time, I didn't think much of these small developments, they merely felt like slightly improved flotation devices that I could hold onto. So you can imagine my surprise the day I was struck with an odd sensation. There was a lightness about me, something I hadn't felt in a very long time. I noticed that my thoughts had become more helpful, more grounded, and less scary. And when anxiety did come up, I found I was recovering more quickly. There was a calmness about me—like the first few moments after the end of a coastal storm, the waves finally relaxing as the sky clears above.

I remember thinking to myself, Huh! I haven't felt this good since I was a young girl. What the hell happened? Day after day, for years, I had been kicking and fighting and shaming myself, gripping onto sinking objects, lost in the deep sea. Now, it seemed, my feet had touched solid ground.

I can say with near certainty that my face turned white the moment I put it all together: my mental health was rehabilitating, and not from one big dramatic event or intervention, but from the small daily practices I was doing on my own initiative. They had snuck up on me, one after another, like fairies slipping through my window in the nighttime and sprinkling magic dust over me as I sleep. This marked the moment I understood the power of daily practice.

My commitment to daily practices grew into something I never could have anticipated, far beyond mental health and into the emergence of *me*. I am becoming my true and authentic self. I pick wildflowers on mountain trails and skinny-dip at dusk. I dine—with myself—at restaurants, and wander through new towns and cities, popping into art galleries and cafes. I take myself to retreats, writing workshops, poetry shows, and overnight getaways. I hire people to help me understand my pain, to guide me into my darkest corners, the spaces I've been most frightened of. I journey through meditation and travel. I grow my business and I write.

I have fallen in love with this raw and real version of me. I have fallen in love with my life, not because it's perfect, but because it's *mine*. And it only gets better as I lean into daily practices that serve my well-being.

That breakdown, in the counselor's office back in 2018, was the storm that birthed the first droplet, the first of my daily practices, the missing ingredient that is now creating the ripples my life is today. My hope is that this book guides *you* toward *your own* personal freedom. That you know you aren't alone. That there are solutions for you. And that your life grows beyond your wildest imagination.

Let's start here, together.

THE POWER OF DAILY PRACTICE

The reason daily practice holds so much power is because of a wondrous thing called *neuroplasticity*. Your brain is programmed to adapt, learn, and change. This is its job. And it doesn't stop evolving once you become an adult. Your brain and nervous system are constantly modifying connections, and these connections either weaken or strengthen depending on how often you use them.

For example, most mornings I do a short yoga stretch flow. For the first couple months of this practice, I watched a video of an instructor who guided me through each yoga pose. Over time, I stopped using the video because I had memorized the sequence. I had created new neural pathways and used them frequently.

Through attention to and repetition of healthy practices, my life began to change. The more I focused on things that felt good, creating new and healthy connections in my brain, the less I focused on the thought patterns and habits that made me feel bad. Over time, the new practices strengthened and the old ones weakened. To put it simply: what you focus on grows.

On average, sixty-six consecutive days of practice are needed for a behavior to become automatic. So be patient. It's tempting to seek a quick fix, a temporary buoy. But I must be honest, I have only found long-lasting solutions with long-lasting efforts. The goal of each daily practice offered in this book is to inspire you to begin the process of creating new and helpful connections in your brain, and for you to remain stimulated and inspired throughout the process.

At first you may notice little to nothing, but as days turn to weeks, and weeks to months, you'll begin to feel the ripples. And once the ripples begin to stretch outward, you'll experience the magic of your brain.

HOW IT WORKS

For quite some time, I didn't know how to describe this book to others. I felt like an awkward high-school senior being asked, for the millionth time, "So what's next?" When loved ones approached me about the book, I'd exhale with a hesitant smile and respond with something like, "Well . . . it's about the power of daily practice. It's more than a book because it has journal prompts and space for daily recordings . . . but it's not a journal, because it has short stories and poetry. It's a hybrid, somewhere between the two, a self-help guide?" I was dissatisfied with this faltering response because I knew this was so much more than that!

A Single Droplet is an interactive book that guides you along small, gradual steps toward your authentic self. I consider the *authentic self* to be a state of wholeness and continuous wonder; where we have acceptance for who we are in this moment *and* embrace our inevitable evolution. Common barriers to living this way include fear, shame, and overwhelm. A way to work through these barriers and receive the gift of authenticity is to read these words *and take actionable steps*, which are, in this case, daily practices. By the end of this process, you will have nourished your well-being to the point where your authentic self can't help but peek through the doorway you've built and walk in as you continue the daily practices on your own.

• • • • •

This journey is eight weeks long, testing out eight different daily practices, one per week. Your days might look something like this: you'll make time for the daily practice you're on, and after you've completed it, you'll record a short entry about the experience. After each week, you will hold space for reflection. You'll then move on to the next week's daily practice. At the very beginning and end of the book are writing prompts, which will show you the way into, through and beyond this journey.

My hope is that, at the end, you will choose to continue working with daily practices, these or others, on your own. Think of these eight weeks as introductory stepping stones: a way to sample different helpful habits and get into the rhythm of new daily practice. Imagine my stories as seeds, the writing prompts as rich soil, and the daily practices as consistent sun and water.

THE DAILY PRACTICES

Week 1 | Connect with Nature
Breathe and get back to your roots.

Week 2 | Physical Movement
Release and strengthen.

Week 3 | Gratitude
Realize and appreciate what you already have.

Week 4 | Mantras
Turn words into reality.

Week 5 | Self-care
Fill your cup back up.

Week 6 | Random Acts of Kindness
Spread your light.

Week 7 | Step Outside of Your Comfort Zone
Empower through curiosity.

Week 8 | Slow Down
Pause and soak it all in.

NOTE TO READER

I went back to talk therapy while writing this book. Sitting with my current therapist, in our first session together, I giggled as I said, "I'm actually writing a self-help book right now." I understood how contradictory this may have sounded—offering guidance as I seek it myself—but I knew how perfect it was to continue my own growth even as I offer a growth opportunity for others.

I am wary of people who stand on their raised podium and claim they hold a secret ingredient, a one-stop shop, guaranteed to cure all ailments and hardship. I am not that person and this is not that book. I believe humans are programmed to continuously evolve; we all seek well-being and will uncover our own concoction of tools and supports as we move forward.

The daily practices inside these pages are broad enough that you can fold them in with your own needs and desires. You may pair them with other tools and supports outside of this book, and you may not. Although this is entirely your choice, I strongly encourage that you access the care you need at any point over the next eight weeks, or beyond, for that matter. These practices will impact your life, but you might receive a great deal more from this book if you combine it with additional support that can help address deeper challenges you may be facing.

I hope this book and these daily practices can be stepping stones that guide you along your path: a new way to approach your mind and calm your nervous system; a door through which to rediscover who you are. Take that first step, and when you get there, take the next. I hope you gain clarity along the way, and I only ask that you take good care of yourself throughout this journey and advocate as you see fit.

And I promise I'll be walking alongside you. Never above or below, but next to you, doing my best to keep moving forward myself, every single day. Sprinkling new droplets, creating new ripples. On and on we grow.

DISCIPLINE DIPPED IN GRACE

If you're like me, you might occasionally fall into the trap of denying who you are right now by fantasizing about who you are striving to become.

I used to imagine my ideal self as a free spirit, a successful entrepreneur, writing throughout the day, eating anti-inflammatory plant-based foods, drinking tea with herbs from the garden and honey from the bees on the property at her dream Vermont home, walking naked through acres of fields with her long untamed hair whipping back in the wind, freckles sprinkled across her sun-kissed skin, picking wildflowers, and traveling the world half the year! I loved daydreaming this version of me: she was calm, interesting, intelligent, confident, wise, and in tune with life. She lived effortlessly, fully, and daringly.

But when I snapped out of this fantasy, I felt low and ashamed. My dream version of myself seemed so far away from reality. I felt pieces inside me that didn't match or belong. I worried I would never live up to her, my imagined highest potential. It wasn't until years into my healing journey that I realized I had it wrong.

We all have some sort of imaginary higher version of ourselves, whether it revolves around our career, body, relationships, life experiences, whatever. Somewhere in this process, we label our current selves *less than* the ideal, or *worse*, we label our current selves *wrong*. Ironically, this only slows down our evolution toward the version of ourself that we long for! In other words, we can't become the person we want to be if we aren't accepting who we are right now. Funny how that works.

So maybe you've felt glimmers of this higher self in the past, but life has wedged its way between you two. Maybe you see a bright, full version of yourself somewhere in the future, but you're not so sure who you are right now. Or maybe you have no idea what your higher self looks or feels like. That's okay too. Wherever you're at, whoever you are now, is fine, even better than fine. It's where and who you're meant to be right now. *Here and now* are the only place and time to begin, we cannot skip or jump ahead of ourselves.

Each moment you show up for yourself and meet yourself exactly where you are, you practice radical self-acceptance: you give yourself *grace*. This is a gift we all deserve, *especially* on our harder days. It is how we combat the black hole of perfectionism and enter a present—and, dare I say, perfect—state of who we are right now.

This journey also requires a special type of discipline. Not one that feels intense, like pressure, full of rigidity, comparisons, and bars set too high. In this case, discipline means *devotion to practice*.

There will be days over the next months when you feel like everything is flowing in your favor, when you're crushing the practices, and life in general. On these days, throw on a fun song and dance in celebration!

There will also be days when you wake up late and rush out the door, when you feel depleted, annoyed, uninspired, and everything is just clunky. These are the days you give yourself extra compassion, and let even the smallest, simplest, shortest daily practice be as significant as one on your best day.

What's important here is that you *do something*. For example, one day you only find a minute to run outside and bury your feet in the cool earth or look up at the stars. Another day you wake up early for a sunrise hike and soak up every sound, smell, and sight. Both of these days matter and are worthy of celebration, because you took action. And if you miss a day altogether, write that down in your daily entry, along with "I forgive you," and then show up the next day.

So just to be clear:

1. Meet yourself exactly where you're at. This version of you, right here, right now, is the *only* place to begin. Everything starts from this moment, but we must be *in this moment* for things to start.
2. *Something* is better than nothing. You cannot mess this journey up unless you stop it altogether. Be realistic with your days; one minute is better than zero. Part of the practice is *getting into the practice!*

Here's your first assignment: pause, and find a way to hold onto these three statements:

I meet myself exactly where I am.
I give myself the grace to take imperfect action forward.
Something is better than nothing.

Write them down and place them somewhere highly visible, where you'll see them multiple times a day. Maybe you'll create a homemade bookmark and stick it in the book you're currently reading, write them on your bathroom mirror, record yourself saying them out loud and set it as your morning alarm, or make a screen saver for your phone or computer. Or, maybe you'll do what Jake and I often default to: a sticky note on the wall.

Seeing these three sentences will act as helpful reminders, and over time, they'll seep into your mind and body. Ultimately, they will influence the way you go about your days, just like the daily practices. Imagine what your life would look like with discipline dipped in grace.

I meet myself exactly where I am.
I give myself the grace to take imperfect action forward.
Something is better than nothing.

BEFORE WE START: SET YOUR INTENTION

Let's get clear about *why* you are going on this eight-week journey. Your *why* is the mental backbone behind many of your accomplishments and a compass for your mind. It can carry you forward, upright and unwavering, through great challenge. We can be mistaken thinking that the difficulty level of something is the determining factor to our failure or success. I believe, that with a strong enough *why*, we are capable of even the most grueling and demanding goals.

I recently watched a documentary that included Patrik Baboumian, recognized as one of the strongest people in the world. It showed an unbelievable moment when Patrik flipped a car on his own. Truthfully, I wasn't interested until he shared the significance of that moment in an interview. When he was a young boy, his parents and sister were in a devastating car accident. Only his mother survived. Since that day, he has aspired to feel hero-like, to get to a point of superhuman physical strength so that he could save someone's life if needed. That is his *why*.

We won't be flipping any cars during the next couple of months, but we will be trying to show up daily and establish new practices. Resistance will undoubtedly make an appearance, and when it does, you'll need to remind yourself of your *why*.

Here's your second assignment: take some time to go through the following steps to establish your reflection space, clarify your *why*, and write your letter of intention.

i. Settle in with this book or a journal. Find a space that offers minimal distraction, somewhere you feel safe and relaxed. Then, find a way to get cozy. Maybe you want to make some tea, grab a blanket or pillow, play soft music, or light a candle. Do what feels best here. You may decide to return to this space for your daily entries or reflections throughout the next couple of months, so take the time to make this a supportive environment.

ii. Now imagine someone on the sidelines of a marathon, finally getting a glimpse of their loved one jogging in the race. For just a few moments their eyes lock, and the partner on the sidelines can see the spirit fading from their marathoner. So they scream and yell and holler all sorts of words of encouragement and remind their loved one *why* they entered that race and *why* they trained for all those months.

    The runner sees the fire in their partner's eyes and hears their shouts. In this instant, they suddenly remember *why* they have been so determined to do the damn race! They remember the feeling, the longing, the desire to start *and* complete this goal. They are reminded that the race symbolizes something much bigger, something that will carry ripples far beyond that day. With this re-grounding, they look ahead fiercely, pick their feet up a little higher, and keep going. The runner is *you*. The loved one cheering the runner on is your letter of intention, also you.

iii. Reflect on your personal and present *why* for committing to the next eight weeks of daily practices. Consider the following questions to get your wheels turning:
- Why were you drawn to this book?
- What have you been struggling with or wanting more of?
- What do you want to learn to let go of?

- What do you want to cultivate within yourself?
- Can you come up with one word or phrase that describes how you want to feel?
- Why is *now* the right time to do this?
- Why should you keep going all the way to the finish line?

iv. In your journal or in the designated space below, with that *why* in mind, begin writing your letter of intention. Take up as much or as little space as you'd like.

v. Revisit this letter whenever you like, but especially on days that feel hard or when your spirit feels like it's fading. Your words will weave through the next few weeks like that loved one on the sideline, giving you incentive and cheer. Make sure to revisit your letter frequently.

WEEK ONE

Connect with Nature:
Breathe and get back to your roots

I walk away

From the noise

The clutter

The worries, complications

The doing and forcing

Each footstep lighter as I near the wooded trail

Stepping underneath the canopy of forest

Through the shadow of trees

Golden hour sending brushstrokes across the darkening path

Slipping off my sandals, leaving them behind

Pine needle, loose twig, and uneven earth beneath my feet

My legs pause on a soft patch of soil

Anchored, as if roots have grown from beneath my soles

Eyes softly close as my head tilts toward the sky

Out of my mind and into my body

I have longed for this

The dense air filters through me as my lungs expand my rib cage

A million crickets harmonize in song

A bird spreads its wings above

My body,

Turning to statue in the midst of creation and life

My mind,

Remembering what always seems to drift away

    That I am no different

        I am built from the same matter

            I require sunlight, water and air

                I am no exception to pain nor imperfection

            I *too* am nature

• • • • •

Nature has been embedded into my days since childhood. Growing up in a small town in rural Vermont required self-made entertainment, and for me and my two brothers, this meant getting outside and finding something to do. In fact, our parents demanded this, locking us out of the house on summer days, forcing us to go to swimming lessons in the pouring rain, taking us hunting at dawn, and limiting computer and TV time to weekends.

I remember wrapping myself in the hammock hanging between two trees in the left corner of our yard, imagining I was inside a cocoon, peeking through the thin cloth up at the trees. My brothers and I made "soup" out of dirt and hose water, swam in the nearby pond, and raced our bikes up and down the neighborhood streets. When I was upset, I'd take refuge in the old cedar tree in front of our home; this tree felt more like an old friend as I perched inside of her, high above everything else. As an adult, my relationship to nature has not changed. It has always been an outlet for me to connect with my body, my mind, and with life at whole.

Whether you grew up immersed in nature or not, this week is an opportunity to relearn how you connect with it. I intentionally selected this as the very first practice because it is revitalizing to be reminded that we too are animals, not above or below the rest of creation, but rather a piece of it. And when we allow ourselves to go back to our roots, simply by stepping outside, we taste our instinctual selves again.

Throughout the three hundred thousand years that *Homo sapiens* have been in existence, our evolution has taken place in the outdoors. Our wiring is intricately woven with nature. Our brains developed while foraging, hunting, migrating, and falling asleep under the stars. As society industrialized, we have found ourselves indoors, detached from nature more and more. In recent years, as the pace of technological evolution has sped up, we sit and stare at screens, from the moment we wake until the time our eyes flutter asleep. We eat lunch with the company of our phones, and put speakers over our ears as we exercise in gyms and move through the streets and park trails, blocking out our natural environment. We select our food beneath fluorescent lighting as we walk up and down the scentless aisles in grocery stores. We run from place to place, with heat or air conditioning blasting at our skin, speeding past breathtaking sunsets, remarkable wildlife, and glimmering streams. We have become disconnected from the very thing our evolution is based upon.

In 1984, Edward O. Wilson introduced us to his *biophilia hypothesis*. The Latin roots of *bio* and *philia* are *life* and *love* – *biophilia* means love for life. Wilson's theory explores the innate attraction we humans have for nature. He argues that humans feel an instinctive pull toward nature and life because humans *are* nature and life. That is why we crave sunshine on our faces and enjoy taking fresh air into our lungs. It is why we stop what we're doing to watch wildlife or close our eyes when listening to the deep rumble of the ocean. It is why we suddenly become inspired or find clarity when deep in the woods or by a body of water. And why we ponder the mystery of life and our part in it all. We cannot separate ourselves from the very thing we are derived from.

By understanding the *biophilia hypothesis*, we can make sense of the research supporting the relationship between well-being and connecting with nature. In an American Psychological Association (APA) article, Kirsten Weir examines some of the benefits we can cultivate simply by stepping outside and connecting with whatever nature is around us: "From a stroll through a city park to a day spent hiking in the wilderness, exposure to nature has been linked to a host of benefits, including improved attention, lower stress, better mood, reduced risk of psychiatric disorders and even upticks in empathy and cooperation."[1] Weir also refers to a study[2] about the impact nature can have on our overall feeling of purpose. "In a meta-analysis, Alison Pritchard, PhD, ABPP, at the University of Derby in England, and colleagues, found that people who feel more connected to nature have greater *eudaimonic* well-being—a type of contentment that goes beyond just feeling good and includes having meaningful purpose in life."

I believe that vital minds and bodies require intentional time with nature. When we do this, we not only calm our physical and mental selves, but we discover an ancient sense of curiosity, aliveness—*biophilia*—beneath our surface. We guide ourselves back to who we are at the very core, feeling a oneness we didn't even know we were missing, and stepping into the present once again. From this space, we can see clearly and feel fully. This is where we find peace, and we must cultivate peace first. We must get back to our roots.

How to Connect with Nature

There are infinite ways you can connect with nature this week. You may know exactly what you want to do or you may have no idea. Wherever you're at is completely right because there is no right way here! The key is letting each daily practice in nature be simple, enjoyable, and intentional:

---

[1] Kristen Weir, "Nurtured by nature," Monitor for Psychology, 51, no. 3, April 1, 2020: 50: access July 2023, https://www.apa.org/monitor/2020/04/nurtured-nature

[2] Pritchard, A., Richardson, M., Sheffield, D. *et al,* "The Relationship Between Nature Connectedness and Eudaimonic Well-Being: A Meta-analysis," *Journal of Happiness Studies,* 21, (2020): 1145-1167, accessed July 2023, https://doi.org/10.1007/s10902-019-00118-6

- **Let it be simple:** Let this practice be uncomplicated and realistic in your day; do not let your mind convince you that in order for this to work you must go somewhere new and exciting and spend a long time there, time that you may not have! A few minutes in your yard or out on your balcony or next to the nearest tree or body of water will do.

- **Let it be enjoyable:** Let this be fun and pleasurable! Allow yourself to play as you did when you were a child: call back to an owl, try to catch a frog, feel the air brush across your face as you skip. Let nature create a spa-like experience: bury your feet in the warm sand, listen to the rain hitting your windows, let yourself melt onto the ground as you look up at the sky, see what images you can find in the clouds or constellations.

- **Let it be intentional:** Let yourself go outside without distractions. No buzzing phone or excited dog or adorable, talkative child. Slip out the back door and stand in the sunshine as you dig your feet into the earth. Escape for a minute; hit Pause. Notice what is happening around you, study the movement of a bug, feel the soft petals of a flower, or listen to the peaceful sound of leaves blowing in the wind. Notice your existence inside this larger existence. Be with yourself and with nature for a moment.

You'll know you're doing this right if you notice something you never did before, whether it be outside of yourself, like a nearby plant or a species of bird, or part of yourself, like the way your feet tingle or wiggle happily in the grass, or the soft smile that grows across your lips as your face shines in the sun. Another way you'll know you're doing this right is if you feel more present: your problems, tasks and worries quiet; a playful childlike energy bursts inside your chest; your breath draws in more deeply; a sense of relief or relaxation washes over you as you let nature seep in. Another way you'll know you're doing this right is if you're simply doing it.

Before you decide how to practice connecting with nature each day, you may want to consider the following questions:

1. How can I make this simple?
2. What sounds enjoyable right now?
3. What needs to happen to make this intentional?

List of Ideas

- Sit or lie somewhere outside
- Feel the branches, leaves, or petals of a plant
- Wiggle your bare feet in the earth
- Observe an insect, bird, fish, or other wildlife
- Close your eyes and listen to the outdoor elements
- Watch the sunrise or sunset
- Garden, forage, or hunt
- Stand at the edge of a body of water
- Sit by a campfire
- Stargaze
- Climb a tree

Daily Entries

Each day, you'll record your daily practice by jotting down a word, sentence, or paragraph, or even drawing a picture. How you capture each practice is entirely up to you! Try to find a consistent time in your day to log your entry. Keeping this book or journal somewhere visible (e.g., near the coffee machine, on your nightstand, with your yoga mat, in your car, next to your laptop, etc.) will help remind you to make your daily entry.

Remember . . . something is better than nothing. We're here to give ourselves grace by taking imperfect action forward and by meeting ourselves exactly where we're at. As long as you keep coming back, you're doing it right.

Day 1

Day 2

Day 3

Day 4

Day 5

Day 6

Day 7

Week One Reflection

You've completed week one! For many, the very start of something new feels the hardest, which is why the completion of this week is such a big deal! The momentum has officially begun, and your brain is waking up to the rhythm and benefits of a new daily practice. Before you dive into week two, take a moment to reflect. I find that we often forget to acknowledge accomplishments, or we rush through celebrations, eager to get to the next thing. Take a moment to savor *this* moment.

Bringing this book or your journal, establish a cozy space to spend the next few minutes. Maybe you'll go back to the very spot where you wrote your letter of intention. If not, make sure your new location feels supportive and comfortable. Maybe you'll play soft music in the background, light a candle, or grab a pillow to wiggle into the present with. Allow your practices to ritualize through these subtle preparations. Take as much or as little time as you'd like. You can't get this wrong as long as you're doing it in a way that feels good for *you*.

Here are some questions to get your wheels turning. Feel free to use them or not.

- What surprised you?
- What did you learn about yourself?
- How do you feel now compared to day one of connecting with nature?
- What did you especially enjoy?
- What do you want to hold onto?
- How did this week support or relate back to your letter of intention?

WEEK TWO

Physical Movement:
Release and strengthen

I used to feel trapped,

Inside of *you*

Cheeks burning

Throat locked

Chest tightly swaddled

Eyes sunken to the ground

I egged you on

I *wanted* to fight you

And I tried

With ruthless criticism

And unfair expectation

Day after day

It was like we were in a boxing ring

And no matter how many times I hit you,

You would stand back up and open your arms to me

And over time, *you* wore me down

I began to see

Your beauty

Your resiliency

Your loyalty

And once again,

Just like when we were little,

We became unstoppable

Climbing mountain peaks

Skinny dipping at dusk

Dancing together in the kitchen

Synced up like childhood friends

Interlaced matter and spirit

Reunited, at last

• • • • •

In middle school, I developed an eating disorder that would last over a decade. From severe food restriction to binging and purging to body dysmorphia, I've been down these winding dark paths many times. Naturally, my relationship with exercise turned abusive too. I became just as obsessed with burning calories as I did with counting them.

Today, I feel fortunate to tell you, I have healed considerably, more than I could have imagined possible. I eat to enjoy food and to fuel myself, and I don't force my body to move when it asks for rest. When I do exercise, I feel empowered as I strengthen my muscles and mind. I even become inspired as I hike forest trails, and feel like a kid again as I dance down hilltops among wildflowers. My heart sings as my feet barely touch the summer grass while dancing to live folk music. My mind settles as I meander through the forest so slowly that I notice the morning dew hanging off pine needles. It's these active moments that make me feel most alive and authentically my own. I *get* to live inside of this living and breathing vessel; it was created for *me.*

To achieve this point of mental and physical freedom has required many years of healing, support from therapists and loved ones, and cultivating a healthy lifestyle. I *still* find opportunities to heal, seeking ways to unite my mind, spirit, and body even more. I have learned to appreciate this difficult experience because I would have never come back home to myself in the way that I have without it. I wouldn't have learned self-love so fiercely. I wouldn't have realized my own grit and potential. I wouldn't understand the sweetness of playing again or the peace of lying on my couch midday with a cup of tea. My healing journey has gifted me with an infant-like lens, an opportunity to experience my body as if it were for the first time.

Beyond the potential healing this week may bring for you, I want to address the indisputable benefits of being active, starting with the obvious: physical movement leads to physical wellness. A Center for Disease Control and Prevention article "Benefits of Physical Activity" explains that "being physically active can improve your brain health, help manage weight, reduce the risk of disease, strengthen bones and muscles, and improve your ability to do everyday activities."[3] Exercise not only helps us feel strong and healthy in current time, but is a way we can positively impact *how* we age.

Physical movement can also help alleviate, manage, and prevent mental health challenges, such as stress and anxiety. These mental agitations can translate into physical discomforts or concerns, showing up as muscle spasms, headaches, fatigue, digestive issues, rashes, chest pain, weakened immune system, and poor sleep, just to name a few. When we activate our body, we release endorphins, which play a key role in mood enhancement and stress and pain control. In addition, by completing an exercise, we gain a sense of accomplishment, boosting our self-confidence and motivation to continue making healthy choices for ourselves.

The Mental Health Foundation's article "How to look

---

[3] "Benefits of Physical Activity." Center for Disease and Prevention. Accessed July 2023. https://www.cdc.gov/physicalactivity/basics/pa-health/index.htm#:~:text=Being%20physically%20active%20can%20improve,activity%20gain%20some%20health%20benefits

after your mental health using exercise" explores this idea: "Participation in regular physical activity can increase our self-esteem and can reduce stress and anxiety. It also plays a role in preventing the development of mental health problems and in improving the quality of life of people experiencing mental health problems."[4] Think of physical movement as an outlet for the body to release what it's holding onto, and a way to uplift the mind and spirit.

Whether you use this week to focus on healing, physical strength, or mental health, see if you can find a way to receive the offerings that physical movement wants to gift you. Feel your mind and body connect once again. Remember and cultivate the strength you carry in your muscles and your mind. This is an opportunity for you to put on a new lens, a lens of curiosity, and see what you can gain from physical movement.

How to Practice Physical Movement

Just like our brains evolved to learn, adapt, and grow, our bodies evolved to move and strengthen; exercise is deeply instinctual. Since many of us no longer gather and hunt, it is our responsibility to continue honoring our body's need and desire to stay active. And doing it in a way that feels best to our unique selves, this will look different from person to person. Use this week as a way to honor the season of life you're in right now.

To be clear, this week is ALL about:

---

[1] "How to look after your mental health using exercise." Mental Health Foundation. Accessed July 2023. https://www.mentalhealth.org.uk/explore-mental-health/publications/how-look-after-your-mental-health-using-exercise#paragraph-18511

- Continuing your healing journey with your body and finding support if needed.
- Strengthening your physical self.
- Moving and releasing stored tension.
- Getting the happy hormones flowing!
- Empowering your mind and body.
- Discovering how you enjoy moving your body.

This month is NOT about:

- Burning calories.
- Losing weight.
- Comparing yourself to others.
- Looking a certain way.
- Being critical of your body.
- Setting unrealistic or harmful expectations on yourself.

• • • • •

Note: If you are on a healing journey with your body, perhaps this week will be of some assistance. However, if it feels too hard, please find yourself appropriate support (e.g., a good friend, a therapist, a different self-help book, a guided meditation, a group class, a walking buddy, a qualified health coach, etc.).

One of my greatest mentors, Adrea Peters, insists that we be our own heroes. What I believe she means by this is that we learn how to take radical responsibility for our lives, to unveil our authentic selves, and then honor the hell out of them, all while trusting that everything on the outside will fall into place. When we walk these bold paths, we will hit points where we need support. Part of being our own hero is advocating for ourselves. Please do that this week, if needed, and any other time throughout this book—and beyond.

List of Ideas

- Walk
- Dance
- Yoga
- Hike
- Swim
- Qi Gong
- Rollerblade
- Workout Class
- Play an active game (e.g., tag, basketball, dodgeball, Frisbee, etc.)
- Climb stairs
- Bike

Daily Entries

Day 1

Day 2

Day 3

Day 4

Day 5

Day 6

Day 7

Week Two Reflection

All I can hear right now is the song *Girl on Fire* by Alisha Keys. Maybe throw the song on and do a little dance? Completing this week is worthy of celebration because physical movement is hard, both mentally and physically. And you've now got momentum with a daily practice! At this point, your brain expects to keep moving forward in this eight-week journey. You are on your way to creating new neural connections.

Before you flip the page to the next practice, let's hit Pause and reflect. Making time and space for reflection is just as important as the daily practice. There are insights and bits of wisdom that float to the surface when we give ourselves the space to stop for a moment: information that could give us clarity about ourselves or a stronger sense of willpower to keep moving forward. Without intentional reflection, these important bits of wisdom may sink back below the surface.

So, let's take the time. Head over to your established cozy space, or make a new one. Then dive into week two reflection, using these prompts if you'd like.

- What surprised you?
- What did you learn about yourself?
- How do you feel now compared to day one of physical movement?
- What did you especially enjoy?
- What do you want to hold on to?
- How did this week support or relate back to your letter of intention?

WEEK THREE

Gratitude:
Realize and appreciate what
you already have

Just for a moment, let go
Of your dreams, ambitions, desires
Of all the things you don't have but long for
And the things you wish away

For just this moment
Stop imagining what your life could be,
So that you may see what *is*

Blinking slowly,
Scanning your surroundings . . .

Your loved ones
Your home
The tree you see from the window

Looking around,
As if you were witnessing your life
For the first time

Just for a moment

• • • • •

I have these moments when everything slows down. It's kind of like a dramatic movie scene when the character hears and sees everything in slow motion, when seconds feel like minutes. In my case, the slow motion happens during the most ordinary moments. Like when I'm walking my dog, Ziggy, in the early morning and am struck by the sight of the gigantic maple tree that we pass by every day. Or, while I'm lying in bed next to Jake at night and suddenly feel this wave of thanks wash through my whole body, as if this normal moment is a rare gift.

And just as soon as this rush of gratitude comes, it leaves, filling me with peace. It's these moments when my eyes unglaze and life is so magnified that I can't help be anywhere but inside the bliss of my current reality.

I haven't always experienced these slow-motion moments. Back in my mid-twenties, I remember desperately wanting to feel peace, but I kept tripping over the life that I didn't have. Nothing ever seemed to be enough; I was always chasing something better, just out of reach. This tormented me, making me feel as if I had been split into two halves that battled one another day after day. This mental state scared me and felt destructive.

Underneath this commotion, however, there was a wise knowing, asking me to find a way to appreciate the life I already had. So I decided one day to begin every day with gratitude for something in my current life, either by writing it down in my journal or saying it out loud in my car while driving to work. To be honest, it felt a little fake at first. The dissatisfied thoughts were still so powerful, constantly judging and comparing, making me question if I was truly grateful or forcing something that shouldn't be there. It was an awkward phase, like a baby giraffe trying to keep up with its mother on its long, new legs. But as time passed, I also became steadier.

Regardless of the discomfort, I kept going, and over time, the practice began to sink in, rewiring my brain to notice and receive things to be grateful for. Things that are already here, that I genuinely appreciate and love. After practicing gratitude for years, I no longer find myself reaching out for these slow-motion moments. Instead, they find me.

Gratitude is a practice that spans across religions, continents, cultures, and medicine. According to a study published in *Psychiatry (Edgmont)* and shared by the National Library of

Medicine, gratitude is ". . . the appreciation of what is valuable and meaningful to oneself; it is a general state of thankfulness and/or appreciation."[5] There is a vast amount of research linking the benefits of gratitude to both physical and mental health. A Mayo Clinic Health System article "Can expressing gratitude improve your mental, physical health?" refers to gratitude as "a magic pill" and says that "expressing gratitude is associated with a host of mental and physical benefits. Studies have shown that feeling thankful can improve sleep, mood and immunity. Gratitude can decrease depression, anxiety, difficulties with chronic pain and risk of disease."[6]

This week, we will use gratitude to strengthen our mental and physical health, and establish a mentality of acceptance for our current life. This new practice will teach the mind that there are slices of contentment available right now, aspects of our lives that are already good as is. Find these and let them anchor you. Over time, you'll notice that gratitude will give you a fresh lens to see through, to discover magic in the mundane, beauty in the ordinary. Like waving to your neighbor as you leave your house in the early morning, or catching the final moments of the sunset during your commute home. Cracks of light can always be found. It's these very cracks that may hold the secret ingredient to your deepest desires. All you need to do is look.

---

[5] Randy A. Sansone, MD, and Lori A. Sansone, MD. "Gratitude and Well Being," *Psychiatry (Edgmont)*, 2010 Nov; 7(11): 18-22, Accessed July 2023. https://www.ncbi.nlm.nih.gov/pmc/articles/PMC3010965/

[6] Amanda Logan, C.N.P., "Can expressing gratitude improve your mental, physical health?" Speaking of Health (blog), Mayo Clinic Health Systems, December 6, 2022. Accessed July 2023. https://www.mayoclinichealthsystem.org/hometown-health/speaking-of-health/can-expressing-gratitude-improve-health#:~:text=Expressing%20gratitude%20is%20associated%20with,pain%20and%20risk%20of%20disease

How to Practice Gratitude

Over the next seven days, you have the opportunity to explore *how* you enjoy practicing gratitude. This may involve a journal, a dinner conversation, a guided meditation, or just a set time when you spend a few minutes witnessing your life. You may prefer to try something new each day or stick with one method for the entire week. You can't get this wrong if you're showing up, meeting yourself exactly where you're at, and staying curious about what feels best for you. Remember, we're in the beginning phase of establishing new daily practices, so feelings of discomfort or uncertainty are normal and part of the process. It takes time for our brains to adapt to new things. Consider discomfort a sign that you're on the right track. Moments of inspiration are a bonus!

List of Ideas

- Pretend you're seeing your life for the first time
- Make a list of all the things your body does right
- Note every food item in your fridge or pantry
- Thank your bank account as you pay a bill
- Research how other people live across the globe
- List your privileges (e.g., education, legal rights, socio-economic status, etc.)
- Notice what feels safe right now
- Journal prompt: What would you want to do if today was your last day?
- Write a gratitude letter to someone
- Listen to a gratitude meditation
- Watch the film *About Time* directed by Richard Curtis

Daily Entries

Day 1

Day 2

Day 3

Day 4

Day 5

Day 6

Day 7

Week Three Reflection

It is time to go to your established reflection spot, or create a new one. Make sure you are cozy, unrushed, and have a space away from others so that you can focus on yourself. Sometimes we're able to get away from people and distractions, and other times the best we can do is shut a door or put headphones on. Do what you can here and let it be good enough. Meet yourself exactly where you're at right now.

When you're ready, reflect on the past week's practice. Using the below prompts, if you'd like, consider the experience—and the growth—you've had. Invite in this moment of pause so that you may absorb the benefits of gratitude. These pockets of reflection are the pieces of this journey that will carry you forward.

- What surprised you?
- What did you learn about yourself?
- How do you feel now compared to day one of gratitude?
- What did you especially enjoy?
- What do you want to hold onto?
- How did this week support or relate back to your letter of intention?

WEEK FOUR

Mantras:
Turn words into reality

A word is merely a word

Until it is not

Until it is declared

Out loud,

Repeatedly

With emotion

And imagination

Moving away from intangibility

Becoming so real,

You reach your finger out in its direction

As if you could touch it with your bare skin

And this is when you realize

That magic does exist

You've seen it with your very eyes

When words turn to life

• • • • •

There was a time when I commuted to work in the early morning before the sun had risen. It took about forty minutes each way and I decided to use that time to focus on me. My small leather journal would be in the passenger's seat, filled with handwritten poems, mantras, gratitude, and thoughts. I kept it there as a safety net, a reminder to do my morning practices and a place to capture words when they came to me. This small object was a sort of lifeline for my mental health.

One of my morning commute practices was stating mantras out loud. At this time in my life, I had a mantra that held the thing I longed for most: peace. It read: "There is peace in my heart." The day I wrote this in my journal was the day these words became stitched into my cells. Not because it felt like my truth, yet, but because it declared my devotion to feeling this way. I had been through too many years of pain and fear. I was ready to feel peace. I needed it. And I was determined to find it.

So, during my morning commute I would say this mantra three times out loud, pausing between each to imagine what peace looked like for me. I often saw myself deep in the quiet woods, walking through tall trees, sunlight beaming through. I'd call in my five senses, awakening the words in my body, making them feel real.

Days turned to weeks and suddenly I felt something inside. Something foreign, but nice: a soft presence of peace glimmered in my chest. Only later would I realize that peace had always been inside of me, just waiting for an invitation to rise to the surface.

With a little consistency and imagination, words *can* become reality. APA defines *mantra* as "any verbal formula used for spiritual, religious, or meditative purposes to help block out extraneous thoughts and induce a state of relaxation that enables the individual to reach a deeper level of consciousness."[7] APA's definition of *consciousness* is "an organism's awareness of

---

[7] APA Dictionary of Psychology (n.d.). Mantra. In *Dictionary.APA.org*. Retrieved July 2023, from https://dictionary.apa.org/mantra

something either internal or external to itself."[8] Merging these two definitions, we can consider *mantra* a way to use words to access a deeper reality for ourselves.

As we discussed at the beginning of this book, *what we focus on grows*. Mantras are a perfect example of what can happen with repetition and intention. They hold the power of creating a truth that doesn't feel like one yet. Over time, the brain and body begin to absorb what you are telling them day after day. Over time, what you say becomes reality. Let the words in your mantra this week be a gateway to possessing what you desire in your life.

How to Practice Mantras

This week, you will come up with a single statement (see the next section), say it out loud every day at least three consecutive times, and embody it. When I say *embody*, I mean practice *feeling* it. Use your imagination to experience the mantra from different angles. What does it look like? What do you hear? Taste? Smell? How does it feel? Imagine it's a page of a picture book that you've jumped into.

There may be an awkward phase at the beginning of this new practice, when your mind doesn't fully believe what you are telling it. You may feel annoyed, frustrated, or silly. This is a normal part of the process, and why repetition and embodiment are crucial. They give your brain a chance to start building new connections. Stick with it, and over time, you will begin to feel the magic of mantras: when words become reality.

---

[8] APA Dictionary of Psychology (n.d.). Consciousness. In *Dictionary.APA.org*. Retrieved July 2023, from https://dictionary.apa.org/consciousness

Your Mantra

You will create our own personal mantra so I offer no list of ideas this week. Mantras are deeply personal. I would never be able to guess what yours should be; only you know that. You may want to look back at your letter of intention from the beginning of this book. Your mantra could very well tie into your *why*. For example, if your intention revolves around feeling more confident, you may create a mantra that says something like, *I radiate confidence.* Or, maybe your intention is to feel mentally healthier. In this case, you could come up with a mantra that validates your mental health: *I am mentally well. I take good care of my mental health. My mental health gets stronger every day.* No need to overthink. In fact, the simpler the better. Your mantra is already inside of you, waiting for its invitation. When you've got it, write it below:

Daily Entries

Day 1 ....

....

....

....

....

Day 2 ....

....

....

....

....

Day 3 ....

....

....

....

....

Day 4 ....

....

....

....

....

Day 5

Day 6

Day 7

Week Four Reflection

You've officially worked with half of the daily practices in this book! Amazing! At this point in the journey, you're well on your way to creating new neural connections around daily practice. You've established a routine and are committed to moving forward. This tends to be one of the biggest challenges: taking one step forward, then another, consistently, every day. But look at you, you're doing it.

In addition to reflection being a time for insight and inner motivation, it's also an opportunity to celebrate yourself. Take a moment to see all you've done up to this point and allow yourself to be happy, proud, and excited about it! I've noticed, at least with myself, that sometimes when I'm working toward a goal in my own personal development, I can become really serious. And then I have to remind myself that it doesn't need to be a serious process. In fact, what fun would that be? As you reflect for this week, I invite you to get playful, loosen up a little bit! At a minimum, infuse some celebration into this moment— throw a compliment or two at yourself!

So, head on over to your reflection space where you can take a few minutes. Don't forget to get cozy, and when you're ready, begin writing.

- What surprised you?
- What did you learn about yourself?
- How do you feel now compared to day one of mantras?
- What did you especially enjoy?
- What do you want to hold onto?
- How did this week support or relate back to your letter of intention?

WEEK FIVE

Self-Care:
Fill your cup back up

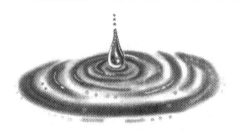

What if you paused?

Just for a minute

Amidst the chaos and disorder

Between the to-dos and cries

To collect yourself

To rest your eyes

To ask what you need, what you *want*

What if you stopped sprinting?

To catch your breath

To eat some food

To ask for help

And then grabbed your empty glass

Walked to the faucet and filled it back up again

· · · · ·

For much of my life, I have considered others before myself. I have let people think I didn't mind doing certain things when I really did. I have committed to plans I did not want to go to. I have taken on more work when I didn't have the time or energy. I have apologized when I did nothing wrong. I have let people cut me off in conversation without attempting to finish what I had planned to say. I have agreed with opinions that make me cringe. I have put others' wishes before my own.

I have also led a busy life with little to no breathing room. I have had to plan months in advance just to see a friend. I've committed to too many responsibilities at once, causing me to crack and break down under the pressure. I've multitasked to the point where I couldn't remember what I had completed. And I've lost memories because my mind was more focused on what I needed to do next than present for the moment.

It wasn't until I established my own self-care practice that I realized I had been people-pleasing and sprinting to the point where I became detached from my own wants and needs. I lost track of the things that kept me going, that made me feel healthy and alive. I found myself depleted of mental and physical reserves, uninspired, and worn out. I had become so distracted by everyone else's lives, and all of my external work, that I quite literally didn't know what to do with myself when I had a spare minute. Uncomfortable and agitated by this free time, I'd quickly fill it in before I could even ask myself what would really nourish me in that moment. Only looking back now can I see how misunderstood I had become to myself.

But as I practiced and developed the skill of self-care, I began to embrace my own moments of refuge. Stopping to drink a tall glass of water as I buried myself in a project. Kindly telling a loved one, "Another day," when they asked to see me and I felt another plan was not the right decision. Scheduling solo getaways to look forward to, something to feed my spirit. Taking a walk, without Jake or Ziggy, giving my entire attention to me. Inside my full and imperfect life, between the to-dos and tasks and social events, I found myself leaning into these quieter moments that felt like air pockets deep in the ocean.

According to the National Institute of Mental Health's Web site, self-care means "taking the time to do things that help you live well and improve both your physical health and mental health."[9] It goes on to say that "when it comes to your mental health, self-care can help you manage stress, lower your risk of illness, and increase your energy. Even small acts of self-care in your daily life can have a big impact." This is something we can do to help us meet our responsibilities and achieve our goals, to grow, and ultimately to thrive.

Over the next seven days, you will practice self-care as a way to fulfill your basic needs to support your physical, mental and spiritual selves. You will examine areas in your life that may need more boundaries; sometimes you don't need to speak your boundaries out loud, sometimes it's a boundary you need to quietly set for yourself. You will respond to your body when it asks to eat, drink a glass of water, or use the bathroom. You will admit when you are holding up too much weight and need some help. You will remember that your mere existence, from the day you were created inside your mother's womb, is enough, and you are unequivocally lovable and worthy. This week, you get to consider decisions that leave you feeling refreshed, full, and rejuvenated. You will create moments that make you sigh out of relief or into relaxation. Moments when your heart beams because you feel like *you* again. *This* is the power of self-care.

How to Practice Self-Care

This week, you will use self-care to fill your physical, mental, and spiritual cups back up. You may notice that your self-care practice affects one of these areas more than the other— this is normal and expected, and is clearly just what *you* need. It's rare that we're ever perfectly balanced.

---

[9] "Caring for your Mental Health." National Institute of Mental Health. Accessed July 2023. https://www.nimh.nih.gov/health/topics/caring-for-your-mental-health

When deciding what to do each day, ask yourself, "What will make me breathe more deeply?" The answer will vary depending on your needs and wants in that moment. Today you may choose to go on a drive alone to clear your head, and tomorrow you may realize you need help from a colleague with a project at work. Other days you may find yourself lying on your kitchen floor for a ten-minute rest.

This is an intuitive practice that will invite you to advocate for yourself. Sometimes this will involve others, and sometimes it'll only require action from you. The key here is to keep things simple. So ask yourself what would help you breathe more deeply, and see what answer comes back.

Ways to practice self-care

- Take a deep breath
- Drink a glass of water
- Delegate or remove unnecessary items from your to-do list
- Say *no* to something
- Spend ten minutes being unproductive
- Take yourself out (e.g., coffee, walk, ice cream, the movies, etc.)
- Write an encouraging letter to yourself
- Go to a creative class (e.g., dance, pottery, paint, etc.)
- Pick yourself flowers
- Get rid of a piece of clothing that you don't feel good in
- Step away from social media for the day

Daily Entries

Day 1

Day 2

Day 3

Day 4

Day 5

Day 6

Day 7

Week Five Reflection

I wish I could sit down and talk with you about this week. I wonder if it was hard, awkward, or overwhelming. I wonder if it was surprisingly easy or just downright enjoyable. I wonder if you learned anything profound about yourself. I wonder if you loved this week or feel like you need a lot more practice with it. Wherever you're at is completely normal and on track.

These practices do so much more than improve our well-being; they help us learn about ourselves. Sometimes it feels great and other times it feels awkward, forced, and uncomfortable. Your experience will be uniquely your own. So take a moment or two to settle into your reflection space, get cozy and invite in a deep breath. When you're ready, using the below prompts, or not, begin your reflection.

- What surprised you?
- What did you learn about yourself?
- How do you feel now compared to day one of self-care?
- What did you especially enjoy?
- What do you want to hold onto?
- How did this week support or relate back to your letter of intention?

WEEK SIX

Random Acts of Kindness: Spread your light

A smile is more than a smile

It is a gesture of kindness

Of love

Connection

Acknowledgement of another's existence

Someone else going about their day

Having their own experience

One that you'll likely never know

Walking swiftly

Passing people by

And for some,

Your eyes meet theirs

Your lips spread upwards

For just an instant

You both respond to one another

Automatically

Naturally

Never knowing who they are

What joys are causing them to beam

And what challenges are weighing on their chest

But you can imagine the ripple effect of a smile

From person to person

Sidewalk to subway

Subway to business

Business to home

It never stops

And it could start with *you*

• • • • •

Random acts of kindness came into my life in my early twenties when I took a graduate psychology course. In the final weeks of this class, we were assigned a group research project, and I just happened to land in the group that chose to study the benefits of random acts of kindness. During the project, we decided that each of us would do an act of kindness on campus.

I'll never forget the thrill and excitement of leaving an envelope with a few dollar bills inside, on the first floor of the library, right near the coffee stand. After carefully placing it against a water fountain, so as to draw attention, I scurried away, passing students and wondering who would be the one to receive it. I imagined what kind of day the receiver was having. Maybe they were missing home or just aced a test! I wondered if the person would pass along the act of kindness, doing something for someone else that week. Regardless of who they were, how they interpreted the envelope, and what they did after, I was just happy to make a fun anonymous connection. It felt so good. It made *my* day.

Since this group project, I practice random acts of kindness regularly. They're why I refuse to buy an E-ZPass. I love paying for the cars behind me at the toll booths. And why I muster up the courage to give unexpected but genuine compliments to people. Even when my heart flutters, or when the interaction feels a bit awkward, I know that I'll leave feeling completely lit up. And I do, every single time.

Before my group project in college, I wouldn't have thought a topic like random acts of kindness would have significant research behind it. But I have been pleasantly surprised. The power behind these acts has major newspapers, universities, scientists, and psychologists talking! Licensed counselor, Steven Siegle, discusses both the physical and mental impacts in his post "The art of kindness" at the Mayo Clinic Health System's *Speaking of Health*: "Kindness has been shown to increase self-esteem, empathy and compassion, and improve mood. It can decrease blood pressure and cortisol, a stress hormone, which directly impacts stress levels. People who give of themselves in a balanced way also tend to be healthier and live longer. Kindness can increase your sense of connectivity with others, which can directly impact loneliness, improve low mood and enhance relationships in general. . . . Physiologically, kindness can positively change your brain. Being kind boosts serotonin and dopamine, which are neurotransmitters in the brain that give you feelings of satisfaction and well-being, and cause the pleasure/reward centers in your brain to light up. Endorphins, which are your body's natural pain killer, also can be released."[10]

Random acts of kindness are not merely something nice to do. Although they are nice, they are powerful moments of connection and vitality for you and the receiver. The impact of such a quick interaction leaves great aftershocks.

---

[10] Steven Siegle, L.P.C. "The art of kindness." *Speaking of Health* (blog). May 29, 2020. https://www.mayoclinichealthsystem.org/hometown-health/speaking-of-health/the-art-of-kindness

This week you get to take the focus off yourself and reflect your light out into the world. I believe random acts of kindness to be one of most important practices in this book because it ties in our common *humanity*. Humanity is measured by our collectiveness. Humans are pack animals; we are social beings; we survive and thrive together, in communities, not alone. We require connection with one another. Random acts of kindness not only benefit your mental, physical, and spiritual self, they do the same for our collective human race, rippling out far beyond ourselves into the lives of others. Connecting you and us once more.

List of Ideas

- Give a sincere compliment
- Pick flowers for someone
- Mail a "just because" letter
- Tell someone something you admire about them
- Leave an encouraging note in a public space
- Leave a positive review for a local business you love
- Donate items you no longer use
- Call a grandparent, or loved one, just to say hi
- Volunteer with an effort that you feel passionate about
- Give your pet some extra love
- Donate to a cause you believe in

Daily Entries

Day 1

Day 2

Day 3

Day 4

Day 5

Day 6

Day 7

Week Six Reflection

I wish I could have been a fly on the wall, watching you spread your light this week, to see your face after each act, and to watch the receiver's reaction to your gesture. Take some time to reflect now, to find a way to hold onto the feeling of giving random acts of kindness for a week. There's some sort of magic to capture here, like trapping fairy dust in a jar. Head on over to your reflection space, use the below prompts if you'd like, and begin writing.

- What surprised you?
- What did you learn about yourself?
- How do you feel now compared to day one of random acts of kindness?
- What did you especially enjoy?
- What do you want to hold onto?
- How did this week support or relate back to your letter of intention?

WEEK SEVEN

Step Outside of Your Comfort Zone: Empower through curiosity

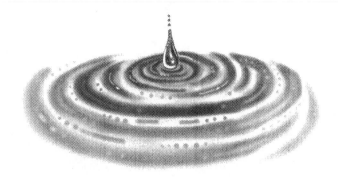

I lie on the hard ground

Stomach chilled from the cool earth below

Shoulders rigid from the wind whipping relentlessly across my back

Knees and elbows ache as gravity pulls them toward a surface that has no give

Arms reach out beyond my head

Chin propped

Eyes fixed

Just inches past my nose,

Between my stretched-out arms

Sits a small, flickering flame

Dancing between bright orange and soft yellow

My hands cup tightly around its edges

Protecting it from all outside dangers

Even my own cautious exhales

The ache in my eyes and skin and joints worth the safety of the little flame

But as time passes, I cannot maintain this statue-like stillness

I am so numb I fear I will slip unknowingly

And where I can feel, the pain is becoming unbearable

Heart skipping, my hands slip and fall flat to the bitter ground

My elbows and shoulders drop in relief

I have lost control

So I lie

After a long while,

I prop my head back onto my chin

Eyes slowly moving toward the small flame

But what stares back at me is not that

Reflecting into my wide eyes is a blaze of fiery red

Crackling with sparks

Wild and alive

I gasp, realizing . . .

That the little flame has been waiting

Waiting all this time,

For *me* to stop protecting it

So that it may grow

So that it can turn to fire

• • • • •

During the summer months, here in Vermont, I often drive myself to the body of water that I grew up swimming in. It's technically a pond, but if you saw its large size, you'd probably think it was a lake. It's beautiful, with trees and rocks surrounding the majority of the water's edge, and a small mountain directly behind it. On the parking lot side, there's a long beach, with a red lifeguard shack. Buoys surround the entire swimming area, indicating the parameters where lifeguards patrol. Within the boundary is ample space to spread out and swim. There must be at least fifty feet from the beach to the buoyed outward edge. But if you want to swim farther distances or escape the playful shouting of the children, you have to cross the ropes, to where the kayakers, paddle boarders, canoers, and occasional snapping turtle venture. Out there, you are no longer watched over; you are alone in the deep water surrounded by trees and rocks and sky above.

I always swam back and forth within the ropes, only crossing them when I was in the company of someone else. But I grew curious of what it would feel like to be out in the open water, at one with nature and myself, away from the buzzing families and flirting teenagers. I imagined how peaceful it must be to be far out away from the world doing one of my favorite things: swimming. But my own imagination held me back; disturbing images would appear in my mind, like bodies floating up to the surface, or some monster pulling me down deep into the water, never to return.

Eventually, my curiosity overrode my fear and I decided to take steps toward swimming beyond the buoys. I remember the first few times, reaching the outer edge where the rope and buoys float, crossing underwater, surfacing back up for air, looking ahead to the end of the pond, and going for it. After a few minutes, I'd turn my head to glance at the people on the beach, now small, and race back toward them. I'd then swim close to the buoys, still on the outer side, but taking comfort in being nearby.

Each attempt, I'd go a bit farther than the last, until I made it across the pond to the rocks that locals call "the ledges." I touched the rock (to make it official), then raced back to the beach, swimming at an impressive pace and feeling a rush of pride and disbelief. I walked out of the water with posture I had never felt before.

You've likely had an experience similar to mine: a time in your life when you've felt equally curious and apprehensive; when you have felt compelled to step outside of your comfort zone. Humans have an intrinsic sense of curiosity because our brains are programmed to solve problems and grow.

However, our brains are also designed to keep us alive. One of the practitioners at Array Behavioral Care, discusses this balance of staying safe and allowing ourselves to expand in their post "The Psychology of Comfort Zones:" "Over a century ago, in 1907, noted psychologist Robert Yerkes told of a behavioral space in which, in order to maximize performance, humans must reach stress levels that are slightly higher than normal. He called this space "Optimal Anxiety," and it's just outside of our zone of comfort."[11]

The article goes on to explain that optimal anxiety reduces as anxiety levels become too high. This tells us that there's a sweet spot, a level of distress that we can grow from, and then a tipping point, after which we no longer gain anything. In my

---

[11] The psychology of comfort zones. *Array Behavioral Care* (blog) (n.d.) https://arraybc.com/the-psychology-of-comfort-zones#:~:text=A%20comfort%20zone%20can%20be,and%20generate%20stress%20to%20a

example of swimming across the pond, I spent multiple days going a little bit farther, until one day I felt confident enough to reach the other side.

When we step outside of our comfort zone, we invite in two unknowns: (1) What will happen if I try? and (2) Who am I on the other side? This is both scary and exciting. This week we are going to practice moving our hands away from the flickering flame inside, so that it may burn brighter. So that *you* may burn brighter.

How to Practice Stepping Outside of Your Comfort Zone

If you're nervous or considering skipping this section altogether, you're probably not alone. This is a very normal reaction— your brain is well intact. If you can, I encourage you to stay, to see what's on the other side of this week. Aren't you curious?

Maybe you've wanted to take a dance class, but feel too out of place or that you've missed your opportunity. Maybe you're interested in learning how to sail, but always push it out of your mind, telling yourself there's no time, money, or way for that to happen. Maybe you've wanted to explore a certain city or town, try a basket-weaving class, sketch the tree in your front yard, take a hiking trip, or see a heavy metal show. Maybe you've daydreamed about flipping an omelet in the air but worry you'll get raw egg all over the stovetop!

Let your curiosity challenge your comfort. Let yourself wonder what it would be like to experience that *thing*, that scary or unfamiliar or ignored *thing*. Let curiosity guide your way and start with the smaller items on your list. No need to go skydiving this week.

List of Ideas

- Go somewhere alone (e.g., class, movies, café, nature trail, etc.)
- Learn a new skill (e.g., cooking, cleaning the dishwasher filter, using the power drill, a new language, etc.)
- Ask someone to hang out with you
- Speak up in a meeting
- Wear something out of your ordinary
- Go somewhere without your phone
- Sing karaoke
- Have someone take a photo of just you
- Ask an "embarrassing" question
- Walk around your home naked
- Flip the damn omelet

Daily Entries

Day 1

Day 2

Day 3

Day 4

Day 5

Day 6

Day 7

Week Seven Reflection

As Jonathan Van Ness, a Fab Five member of the television series *Queer Eye*, would say, "Yass, Queen!" This week may have felt uncomfortable and hard and maybe even bad. It may also have felt cool and fun and inspiring. Perhaps you experienced a combination. Whatever you're feeling here is progress; it's *your* unique path, nobody else's. There are growing pains and triumphs in this journey—we cannot have one without the other. Notice what has come up for you and include all of it in your reflection. Using the below prompts, if you'd like, begin writing.

- What surprised you?
- What did you learn about yourself?
- How do you feel now compared to day one of stepping outside of your comfort zone?
- What did you especially enjoy?
- What do you want to hold onto?
- How did this week support or relate back to your letter of intention?

WEEK EIGHT

Slow Down:
Pause and soak it all in

I was racing to work one day

Hands tightly gripped around the steering wheel

Mind fixated on the day ahead

When something caught the corner of my eye

Turning my head, I saw a large garden next to a small home

And as I looked more intently

I noticed an empty chair

Facing the garden

On the outer edge behind the growing crops

Placed in the very middle of it all

My foot didn't lift on the gas to slow

But it felt as if time had stopped

During those few seconds, I was mesmerized

For the remainder of my commute,

I relished in the idea of the chair

That its only purpose was for someone to sit down and admire
their garden

To make the time to rest as they watch their labor come to life

I want to sit and watch too

• • • • •

If you were to shadow me during the first hours of a new day, you would see me leave the warmth of my bed, drink some water, change clothes, and go outside. We would walk quietly in the woods with Ziggy and maybe Jake. Returning home, we'd enter my studio, a long awkwardly shaped room in the finished basement. There, I would go through my memorized yoga stretches, and then you'd stare, perhaps unenthused, as I sat on a yoga block to meditate. After, I would flip on the lights, set to a soft glow, and free-flow write: a writing practice where I don't let the tip of my pen leave the paper until my thoughts feel complete. You would watch, as I write the date at the top of the page, and then let the words spill out, like honey onto the kitchen counter; my hand moving as my mind makes sense of itself.

> Journal Entry 7.5.2022 *"Soften your face,"* she whispered to me. *As soon as she arrived, she left. Before the words hit my mind, I felt a gentle wave smooth over my face. Skin around my eyes and cheeks. Relaxing in the new state. I often find myself pushing, pulling, yanking, and running. Forcing and controlling; my safety nets. But then I am reminded, over and over again, that everything will happen just so, regardless. That my need to manipulate only uses energy. And that I always have an invitation to soften my face, letting a warm rumble carry through me. A different approach to the same day.*

Before I practiced slowing down, I would wake up at 6:45 A.M., sleep for another five to ten minutes, then run around frantically to be at work at 7:00 A.M. in my home office. I hardly gave myself enough time to throw on a bra, find socks in the dirty laundry, or pee, before opening my work emails. Many of us understand these types of mornings, mornings when all you can think about are the next five things to do before you've even gotten to the first. At that time in my life, slowing down felt impossible, and yet, I knew I needed to make it happen.

According to the Berkeley Well-Being Institute article "Slowing Down: 14 Science-Based Ways to Enjoy Life," "when our minds are speeding, our performance and effectiveness get slower or weaker. It's not 'being slow' that we're seeking necessarily, it's the *feeling* that we have time to do the things that matter. We can handle our daily tasks, we don't feel stressed, and we feel like we have the time to rest, be present, and enjoy the good things in life."[12] From the space of slowing down, of giving ourselves the time to process and experience, we can feel and do better.

The days of haste and multitasking must be addressed if we want to improve our quality of life and overall well-being. And it's not that we need to change our lives, uprooting what we've built, but instead, we can put a little effort into slowing down and infusing our current realities with more intention and thoughtfulness. There is *always* opportunity to slow down, to unweave the tangled plans and to-dos by taking a step back, a moment of pause. Like a repotted plant, you too need space to grow.

How to Practice Slowing Down

This week, you will find pockets of time and space to sink into. Whether it be taking a moment in your car before walking into

---

[12] Tchiki Davis, MA, PhD. "Slowing Down: 14 Science-Based Ways to Enjoy Life." *Berkeley Well-Being Institute* (blog) (n.d.) https://www.berkeleywell-being. com/slow-down.html

work, waking up five minutes earlier to not feel so rushed as you get ready for the day, or shutting your phone off so you can focus better on a project or be more present with someone. These next seven days invite you to use your spare minutes differently and to approach busy times more clearly. I encourage you to cultivate an inner softness, a tender flexibility within yourself that gives you permission to slow down amidst your full life. Despite what the outside world is telling us, there is always more time and space to be found.

List of Ideas

- Put your phone away so you can focus
- Look at the moon before going to bed
- Drive slower
- Minimize multitasking
- Take a bath
- Try a guided meditation
- Practice mindful eating
- Lie flat on the ground for few minutes
- Go to a restorative yoga class
- Observe the slowness of nature
- Read *How to Relax* by Thich Nhat Hanh

Daily Entries

Day 1

Day 2

Day 3

Day 4

Day 5 _____

_____

_____

_____

_____

Day 6 _____

_____

_____

_____

_____

Day 7 _____

_____

_____

_____

_____

Week Eight Reflection

You have officially completed all eight practices in this book. Well done. I want you to go to your established space, get even a little more cozy than usual, and allow yourself to reflect for the final week of daily practice in this book: slowing down. Use the below prompts, or not, and take as much or as little time as you'd like.

- What surprised you?
- What did you learn about yourself?
- How do you feel now compared to day one of slowing down?
- What did you especially enjoy?
- What do you want to hold onto?
- How did this week support or relate back to your letter of intention?

CONCLUSION

I always thought that I needed to let go
To somehow release the worries and fears
The bad habits and unwanted thoughts

But the more I fought, the stronger *they* became
Sending me into a darkening spiral
Of endless suffering

It wasn't until I tried something new,
That I understood
Instead of working so hard to get rid of these pieces,
These parts of me

I softly pivoted my feet and walked in a different direction
Without judgment or resentment, but curiosity
Curiosity to see what else was out there

And the more I focused on what things I could discover
The more I rediscovered,
Me

Finding myself barefoot, wiggling my feet into the cool earth
Stretching my body on a yoga mat in the early morning
Opening my eyes to witness what I already have
Using words to unlock my deepest desires
Taking time for nobody but me
Touching someone's heart with mine
Doing things I never imagined I would, or could
And taking a moment to sit

As time passed, practicing these other pieces of me
I realized that I am uniquely my own
And capable of so much more than I thought

I realized that my greatest achievement in life is *me*
Not the things I've done but rather,
The person who I am

I have given myself the greatest gift anyone could
A chance to rediscover
To uncover
My infinitely evolving
Authentic self

And the funny thing is that it didn't take much
Little to nothing really
Just a bit of discipline dipped in grace
Infused inside the belly of daily practice
Turning from droplet to ripple
Growing beyond itself
On and on, it goes

• • • • •

Letter to yourself . . .

When I attended my first retreat, I was instructed to write a letter to myself on the final day. I still take this very letter out every now and then just to reread it, amazed by the wisdom I had at that time and the growth I've shown since. There is something that happens when you address yourself in a handwritten letter, your words piling on one another, a bundle of compassion, guidance, and reflection. A time capsule for *you*. Right now, you have a great deal of insight and direction to share. It's time to let that voice speak.

First, flip to the beginning of this book, or your journal, where you wrote your letter of intention. Reread this letter, remembering where you were when you wrote it and how you were feeling at the time. Recall at least five details (e.g., what you were wearing, the physical location you were in, what season it was, emotions you were feeling, etc.). Jump back into that moment.

My five details:

1 ....

....

....

2 ....

....

....

3 ....

....

....

4 ....

....

....

5 ....

....

....

• • • • •

Now, find a way to scan through the past eight weeks. Maybe you'll close your eyes, play soft piano music, and imagine this journey as a time-lapse, scenes of a movie, or a slideshow of pictures. Or, perhaps you'll flip through the pages of daily entries and reflections, reminding yourself of the steps taken to get to this point.

Once you feel reacquainted with some of the finer details and highlights, take some time to consider the questions below. You may include the answers in your letter, or they may act as stepping stones for the message that comes through. However long or short, detailed or simple, your letter is uniquely your own, like a fingerprint. Nobody knows what you need to hear except you. Trust this and begin writing.

- How have you grown?
- What pieces of you have remained the same? What pieces have quieted? What pieces have risen?
- What are you celebrating most?
- Did your intention from the beginning of the book develop or change?
- What kept you moving forward?
- Do you want to continue any of the practices?
  - o Connect with Nature
  - o Physical Movement
  - o Gratitude
  - o Mantras
  - o Self-care
  - o Random Acts of Kindness
  - o Step Outside of Your Comfort Zone
  - o Slow Down
- What are you curious about now?

ACKNOWLEDGEMENTS

To Tegan and Kelsey for being my rocks and allowing your artwork into this book (Tegan Coley Photography, Kelsey Telek Art). To Jake, for believing in me, especially on the days when I didn't. To Adrea, for being my North Star at the very beginning of my writing career. To my editor, Linda, for amplifying my voice and taking these words to the next level. To Mary Catherine, for turning this book to life through audio. And to my parents, for reading to me before bed every night when I was a little girl.

Printed in the United States
by Baker & Taylor Publisher Services